Bless Our Pets

POEMS OF GRATITUDE FOR OUR ANIMAL FRIENDS

Poems selected by
Lee Bennett Hopkins

Illustrated by
Lita Judge

EERDMANS BOOKS FOR YOUNG READERS
GRAND RAPIDS, MICHIGAN

To Linda Leone Finch, a true lover of animals
and a wonderful friend.

– L. B. H.

To all the critters who share their love with us.

– L. J.

Contents

Kitten

Small as an orange,
trembling in my hands,
your eyes lantern-bright
open wide with fright.
Poor kitty,
I must be a giant to you,
but I don't growl,
or bite,
or fee-fi-fo-fum.
I'm a good giant who
will feed you,
snuggle you,
pet your fur.
All I want is you
to bless me
with your purrrrrrrrrrrrrrrrrr.

— *Ann Whitford Paul*

Puppy

Those brown eyes, round as chestnuts,
calm me, message me *I love you* without words.
You bark at trespassers: mouse or man,
those who don't belong at my door.

Then, suddenly, your soft snore
fills the room, becomes our special place
as your soft belly warms my bare feet,
tells me stories of puppy love,
sleepy paws, and peace.

— *Rebecca Kai Dotlich*

Goldfish

Pebbles, plants, water moves,
you are the dancer—
your glass bowl, your stage.

I watch you every day,
dancing with you.
You are so shiny, you watch back,

blowing fish kisses,
bobbing up for food,
chasing it when it falls.

We grow together,
my blessed golden one.

You fan the water.
I fan the air.
We dance a prayer.

— *Linda Trott Dickman*

A Prayer for My Gerbil

Watch over every tiny part.
Whatever sniffs
or scurries,
listens,
looks,
waits,
or worries,
hesitates
or hurries.

Her slender tail,
her tender toes,
her whiskered cheeks,
her twitching nose,
her dreaming eyes,
her drumming heart:
watch over every tiny part.

— *Eric Ode*

Prayer for a Parakeet

You live a comfortable life
with a shiny water bottle
and a few plastic toys
to keep you entertained.

You sleep in a cage
so it's hard to believe
your wild cousins flit across
a thick jungle canopy.

Your food comes in a box
yet you once feasted
on brilliant insects
and sweet tropical fruits.

I pray you retain
some essential wildness
no cage can hold,
no one can tame.

— *Ralph Fletcher*

Hamster Hoping

Little hamster,
hiding hamster,
there behind your wheel,
won't you come and say hello?
I'd like to make a deal.
I'll hold still,
speak so soft,
put food upon my hand.
You come closer,
sniff around,
scurry, quest, then stand.
Place your paws upon my thumb,
and if it be your will,
we'll begin our friendship now.
Come here, and eat your fill!

— *Sarah Grace Tuttle*

Lop-Eared Rabbit

Blessed are
the soft of fur,
the long of ear.
I wish you safe
from harm,
from fear.

I wish you
snug,
cozy, warm.
I wish you safe,
curled in my
arm.

Your ears,
dropped down,
surround, embrace
your wide-eyed,
gentle rabbit face.

For from your tiny,
lop-eared start,
your whiskered ways
soon won my heart.

– Joan Bransfield Graham

Dreaming of Savannah

I dream of you in the morning—
I hear a nicker, then a neigh.
Apple? Carrot? Handful of hay?

I dream of you each afternoon—
the velvet softness of your lips,
your breath, warm upon my fingertips.

I dream of you late every night—
glints of moonlight tangle your mane.
We race across the star-strewn plain.

— *Kristine O'Connell George*

A Letter to My Guinea Pig

If I could pick
a pet to pet,
the pet I'd pick
is you.

I miss your friendly,
furry face,
and all your cuteness, too—

those little legs,
that scrunched-up nose,
the squeak that melts
my heart,

your sweet scent
on our sofa,
and your paw prints
on my art.

I long to pinch
those puffy cheeks—
so squishy,
soft, and smooth.

Your licks of love
like summer breezes,
comfort, calm,
and soothe.

I'm grateful for
the endless joy
you bring to
all my friends.

I'll see you soon,
my treasured pal,
the moment
summer camp
finally
ends.

— Darren Sardelli

Box Turtle

Helpless
little turtle
squirming on your back,

wriggling
polka-dotted legs,
tummy, hard shellac.

I place you
on all fours again,
hard dome beneath soft hand.

Your armored plates
so colorful—
your shell a wonderland

of black and orange
markings.
Geometric art

repeats . . . repeats . . .
around your back.
I learn this map by heart.

I'd love to build
a home for you,
but something nags at me.

I pet you
until dinner,
murmur prayers,
set
you
free.

— *B. J. Lee*

Pet Snake?

Thank you for inviting me
to meet your brand-new pet.
I never thought a snake would be
a pet that you would get.

I watch her wrap around your arm.
You stroke her like a cat.
I didn't know a snake would let
you do a thing like that.

I pray some day I'll learn to love
a friendly snake or two.
But heaven knows I'm grateful that—
this one belongs to you!

— *Charles Ghigna*

Mouse Dreams

You are in a cage quietly sleeping
with your tail half-circled around you,
your chin on your little pink paws.

You built that nest, tidily heaping
the shreds that now softly surround you.
You breathe in and out without pause.

But now and then, quite unprotected,
I see your ears twitch. You go tense
and you shudder, as if you are wary

of threat, as you sleep unprotected.
And I wonder: what is it you sense
in your dreams? Is it terribly scary?

Is it snake or hawk or owl?
Is it pounce, or hiss, or growl?

Little mouse, you're safe. Be still.
I'll always be here to take care of you.

I will.

— *Lois Lowry*

Old Calico

Her calico head
lies calmly still
in her same old bed.

Her purrs
now murmurs
of blessed memories—

bouncing toys,
things that skitter,
scratching posts,
catnip-pouncing.

Stretch out, old cat.

You've earned
your rest.

You've been the best.

— *Prince Redcloud*

My Old Dog

Snuggle into me
while I scratch your ears

remembering
so many years
since you were
my precious, tiny pup.

Snuggle,
cuddle up,

let's cherish
the many wondrous
times we have together.

Snuggle, sigh,
dream with me,
old boy.

I'll forever
recall each and every
day
I had with you.

I know you'll forever
remember, too.

— *Lee Bennett Hopkins*

Thanks are due to Curtis Brown, Ltd., for use of "Puppy": copyright © 2024 by Rebecca Kai Dotlich;
"Old Calico": copyright © 2024 by Prince Redcloud; "My Old Dog": copyright © 2024 by Lee Bennett Hopkins.
All used by permission of Curtis Brown, Ltd.

Thanks are also due for commissioned works used by permission of the respective poets, who control all rights:
Ann Whitford Paul for "Kitten"; Linda Trott Dickman for "Goldfish"; Eric Ode for "A Prayer for My Gerbil";
Ralph Fletcher for "Prayer for a Parakeet"; Sarah Grace Tuttle for "Hamster Hoping";
Joan Bransfield Graham for "Lop-Eared Rabbit"; Kristine O'Connell George for "Dreaming of Savannah";
Darren Sardelli for "A Letter to My Guinea Pig"; B. J. Lee for "Box Turtle"; Charles Ghigna for "Pet Snake?";
Lois Lowry for "Mouse Dreams."

Published in 2024 by Eerdmans Books for Young Readers, an imprint of Wm. B. Eerdmans Publishing Co.,
Grand Rapids, Michigan ○ www.eerdmans.com/youngreaders

 ○ Manufactured in China ○ ISBN 978-0-8028-5546-6

33 32 31 30 29 28 27 26 25 24   1 2 3 4 5 6 7 8 9 10

A catalog record of this book is available from the Library of Congress. ○ Illustrations created with watercolor and colored pencil